CW01187110

© 2011 Joseph da Silva

What is a Business Analyst? by Joseph da Silva is licensed under a Creative Commons Attribution-NonCommercial-ShareAlike 3.0 Unported License

This means that you are free:
to Share — to copy, distribute and transmit the work
to Remix — to adapt the work

Under the following conditions:
Attribution — You must attribute the work in the manner specified by the author or licensor (but not in any way that suggests that they endorse you or your use of the work).
Noncommercial — You may not use this work for commercial purposes.
Share Alike — If you alter, transform, or build upon this work, you may distribute the resulting work only under the same or similar license to this one.

http://creativecommons.org/licenses/by-nc-sa/3.0/

Worldwide, there are between five hundred thousand and one million people working as Business Analysts. During just one week in February 2011, there were an average of 800 open vacancies for Business Analysts across the UK.

So why are all types of businesses, from charities to investment banks, hiring so many of them?

The simple answer is because all businesses need to change – regularly – and business analysts enable that change to happen.

But what does that actually entail? What do they actually do?

To answer that satisfactorily needs a little bit more discussion about the complexities of modern businesses, and in particular about the systems that support them. Systems in this context can be organisational, process–driven or IT based – and the business analyst needs to understand all three.

The complications of modern business are diverse – some companies have grown through mergers and acquisitions, inheriting multiple systems from organisations that no longer exist. Other companies have grown explosively from small, two man operations to global powerhouses in as little as 10 years.

This growth comes at a price; business does not always have time to do things "properly". Customers, markets and investors won't wait for you to migrate all your data onto one computer system, to scale up your accounting systems or consolidate your office locations.

They want you to keep going, and keep growing – so you end up running multiple systems, and worry about combining things later.

The problem with this is that the longer you wait, the more complex the problem becomes. Staff double key information into multiple systems, and as you grow you need twice as many of them. Eventually this becomes unsustainable so you decide you have to combine the systems to cut costs.

But where do you start? You can't just turn one of them off – they both contain information that is critical to the running of the business, and they need to be used everyday. And it's not as easy as moving the information from one system to the other as they use different formats and support slightly different processes.

This is where a Business Analyst would come in.

Business Analysts have a specialist skill in being able to understand, abstract and communicate any business problem, in a way that different audiences can clearly understand.

They are experts in understanding the true needs of a business and the impacts arising from a particular problem; they are also experts in expressing this to people who can do something about them.

They help businesses deliver all types of change, not just IT projects.

BAs aren't experts on the detail of your business. They probably don't know the complexities of your sales order processing.

They're not technical experts either – they wouldn't know how to develop code for your payroll system.

But they do know a lot about the entire breadth of business – and about the breadth of systems that support them. And more importantly, they understand enough about both the business and technical aspects of change to act as a bridge between them.

This unique combination of viewpoints couple with analytical and communication skills makes the BA invaluable to any business change team.

In the earlier example of combining multiple systems, the BA would use their investigative and analytical skills in order to answer the following questions:

- WHAT BUSINESS PROCESSES DO THESE SYSTEMS SUPPORT?
- WHAT BUSINESS DECISIONS RELY ON THESE SYSTEMS?
- WHAT DIFFERENT TYPES OF PEOPLE USE THESE SYSTEMS, AND HOW DO THEY USE THEM?
- WHAT BUSINESS INFORMATION DO THESE SYSTEMS CONTAIN?
- WHAT OTHER SYSTEMS RELY ON THESE ONES?
- WHAT VALUE DO THESE SYSTEMS AND PROCESSES ADD TO THE BUSINESS, AND TO THE END CUSTOMER?

These questions are critical for the different roles that will be involved in replacing the system, and each of them can be answered in different levels of detail. One of the skills of a BA is understanding who needs to know these answers and how much detail they need in order to do their job.

Just understanding the current situation isn't enough however. The BA also needs to understand what the desired situation is, and this is more important than you might think.

> *"Just replace it exactly as it was - make it work the same"*

This statement makes a massive assumption on behalf of all the users that the current system works perfectly satisfactorily. Never mind that it might take 10 minutes every time someone wants to run a basic report or that customer addresses are regularly keyed in incorrectly.

This is why understanding the business processes that the system supports is a key first step for the business analyst. The BA is there to challenge the current state in order to get to the root of what the business really needs.

The business doesn't actually need to replace the system "like for like". The business really needs to perform its processes as efficiently and as effectively as possible. There is often a big difference between these two.

The next aspect of the BA role is equally as important; communication.

Just understanding a business problem isn't enough – it needs to be communicated to someone who can do something about it.

Business Analysts are experts in all forms of communication; verbal. visual and textual. BAs will use a range of techniques to express a business need or problem in a clear, unambiguous and verifiable way.

> *"But why do I need someone to do that? Can't I just talk to the solution guys myself?"*

Experience has shown that this is rarely effective. If you've ever struggled to understand a mechanic, mortgage advisor or heating engineer then you may appreciate the problem.

Specialists speak different languages, and have different priorities. A programmer doesn't understand why you gather sales leads in a particular way, and a sales rep doesn't understand how Finance account for his commission.

The BA understands the perspectives on all sides and can explain them clearly and articulately.

Particularly where IT systems are concerned there are many different complexities relating to how that system can perform and what it can do. They can also be very expensive to change, and to support. Changes require extensive testing to make sure that they've been made correctly and that nothing's been broken whilst making that change. So when a business makes a change, it needs to be sure that it's changing the right thing, and it's not always easy to express.

> "I WANT TO LAUNCH A NEW PRODUCT CALLED PRODUCT X. ADD IT TO THE LIST OF OPTIONS ON OUR WEBSITE."

Just giving this to an IT team will probably result in a new option being added..but will anything happen when a customer selects it?.

> *"WELL, OBVIOUSLY, I WANTED AN ORDER TO BE AUTOMATICALLY SENT TO THE FULFILLMENT TEAM"*

Is that obvious? Not necessarily. What about the rules around what types of customer can select it (new customers, existing customers, high value customers...) ? What about the payment options? And how should the accounting team deal with the revenue from this new product?

Giving an IT team a one– or two–line statement rarely provides enough clarity for them to really understand what they need to do, and there is rarely one team involved in making the change. As well as needing to analyse the business need and the implications arising from it, the BA will use different techniques to express it in an unambiguous way.

For example, the steps that a customer takes to log on to a website could be described as:

1. customer inputs their email address and password
2. the system checks the validity of those details
3. the system retrieves that customer's recent orders
4. the customer's orders are presented to them

Alternatively, this can be represented as follows:

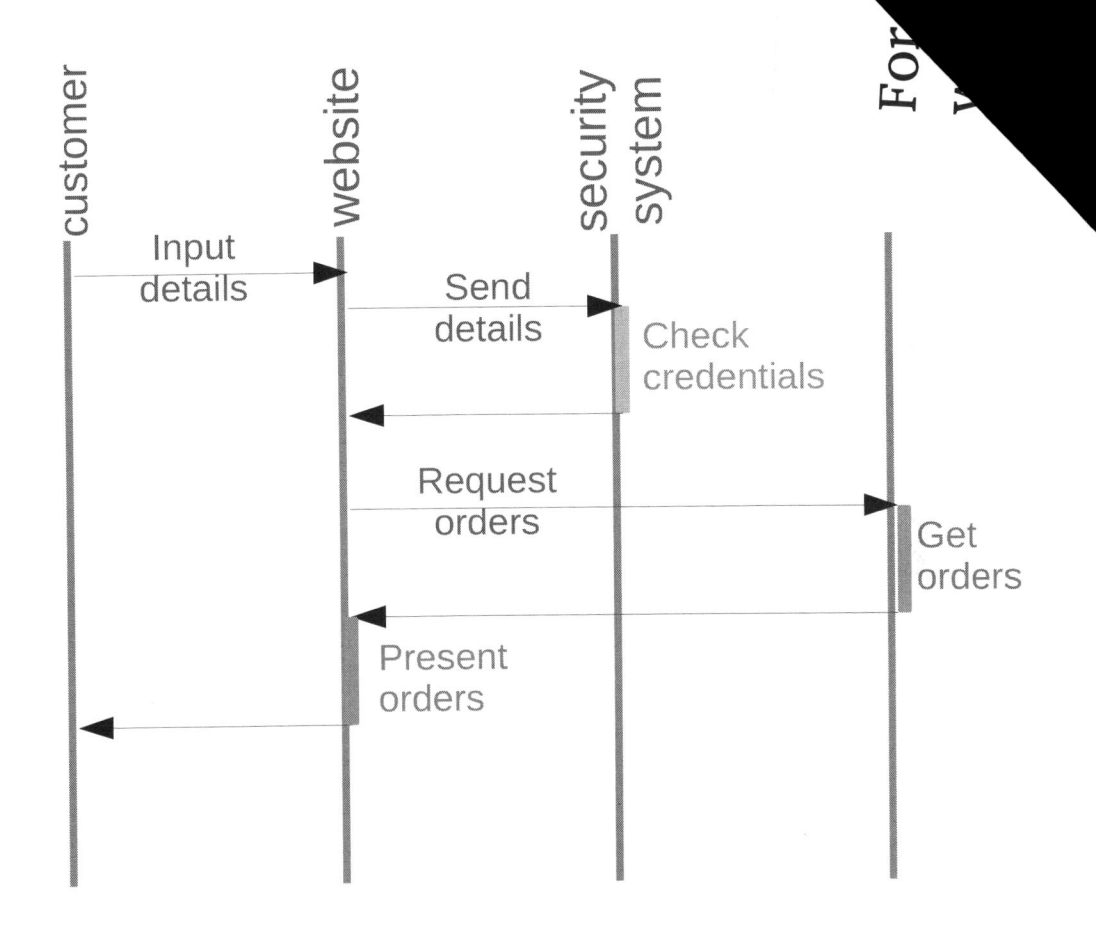

Sequence diagram with lifelines: customer, website, security system, For[...]

- customer → website: Input details
- website → security system: Send details
- security system: Check credentials
- security system → website: (return)
- website → For[...]: Request orders
- For[...]: Get orders
- For[...] → website: (return)
- website: Present orders
- website → customer: (return)

This is a simple way of reflecting a series of transactions and at the same time abstracting out the elements that will be involved; when such a series of transactions runs to 10 steps or more, a diagram such as this is a much more effective means of communication than a numbered list.

teams of people often faced with reams of text, visual representations offer a much clearer, unambiguous representation of what the business really wants.

Another consideration is that the people working on your problem may be geographically remote from you, and may not speak the same day to day language, never mind the same business language. Offshore development teams are increasingly common across all types of business and are likely to continue to grow in use. This can introduce additional barriers to communication, making it even more important that the business' needs are unambiguously represented.

It's not just about what you *think you* want

> *"So you write down what I want and then draw some pictures? Anyone can do that."*

There is a bit more to the BA role than that. A key aspect of the role is getting to the root of what the business truly needs.

> *"I want a monthly spreadsheet of sales by region"*

The real need here isn't for a spreadsheet. The real need is probably to manipulate the sales data, or to generate graphs. Or maybe it's to add in data from other sources.

This may seem pedantic but if it takes another day for the user to manipulate that information then understanding why it's needed may allow a different solution to be produced that saves that time, and therefore saves the business money. For example, a dedicated reporting tool may already exist within the business that will automatically generate the graphs needed.

> *"If I say I want a spreadsheet, then I want a spreadsheet!"*

> *"Maybe you do. But apart from the fact that I won't be doing my job properly if I don't understand the true need behind this statement, you might miss out on a solution that saves you time and money"*

Building what the business truly needs can cost far less than always building what it thinks it wants. And understanding exactly what is needed makes realising and tracking the associated benefit a lot easier.

Business Analysts don't simply ask you what you want. That's part of it, but the added value of the BA comes when they *challenge* what you want and identify other considerations that you might not have thought of.

For example, you might want to launch a new product. So you might need to specify new product codes, perform applicability checks and define a sales commission structure. You might think that would cover everything...

A BA in this situation would be asking questions about the accounting structure of the new product. About the support impacts. About changes to customer correspondence. About changes to management reports. They would also be challenging whether or not a brand new product was actually required, as opposed to configuring an existing one – one answer could be to allow differences in accounting.

BAs approach business problems from a holistic perspective – they see the whole organisation and can assess the impacts of a proposed change across all parts of that organisation.

They're on your side

The Business Analyst is interested in understanding what your needs are and communicating them effectively so that they can be delivered..

On any project, the Business Analyst and the Project Manager should be working as a team, with a healthy, professional tension between them. The PM is responsible for delivering the change, whilst the BA is responsible for that change achieving what the business really needs. BAs have a strong focus on quality and business benefits; PMs have a strong focus on costs and timescales.

BAs should also have a close relationship with their stakeholders in the business, as well as the design, build and test teams. All of these are effectively "customers" of the BA; the business need to be comfortable that the BA has understood and expressed their needs correctly, and the design, build and test teams need to be confident in the completeness, accuracy and clarity of what they're being asked to deliver.

"But we're Agile. We don't need a BA"

Says who? Nowhere in the Agile manifesto does it say *"no business analysts"*.

What it does say is *"[we value] working software over comprehensive documentation"* and in order to get working software, you need to understand and articulate what it is that the software needs to do. That's what BAs are trained to do.

The ability of the BA to understand and express requirements is arguably more valuable in an Agile environment where documentation is kept to a minimum.

> *"But SCRUM says I can talk direct to the developer..."*

And in some situations this is absolutely the best thing to do, and Agile techniques aren't new in this regard. If you're in a relatively small company with no legacy systems (or processes), building on a single platform with few changes happening at once then you probably can talk straight to the developers and get what you want 80–90% of the time. It might be quicker, or of higher quality with a BA., but it's probably good enough.

However, if you have multiple systems, lots of legacy platforms, multiple developments happening at once, multiple departments involved with conflicting needs, high market visibility, 3rd party involvement, offshore development teams – and you have your day job to do as well – then having someone who can understand and express your problem in clear terms to the people who will fix it for you will significantly increase your chances of success and reduce the business risk associated with this change, regardless of the development method being followed.

Where BAs also add value is in assuring that you deliver to the original intentions of the project. By abstracting and expressing your needs in an unambiguous way they can be linked to and tracked against the benefits you've set out to deliver in your business case.

Abstraction is not just about drawing pictures or helping someone unfamiliar with a situation to understand it better.

It's a valuable technique to help everyone involve step back form the day to day situation to remove complications like technology, people and emotions to allow the true business need to be assessed. Focusing on everything at once can cloud the true situation and prevent actual business value from being realised.

> "I haven't got time for workshops and meetings. How about I write my own requirements down and give them to you?"

It's not actually about just writing things down. Although BAs can often be negatively thought of as mere stenographers, there is both an art and a skill to capturing requirements effectively – and bad requirements can be very costly due to the amount of eventual rework involved.

A Business Analyst will seek to understand both what you want and why you want it. This will enable them both to express it clearly and also to assess the impact that it may have on what other interested parties may want.

This is another skill of the BA; they are trained facilitators and can ensure that discussions are held between multiple parties that have an interest in the change being made. Whilst you may have a clear idea of what you want and it may be undeniably useful to you, it might actually cause problems for someone else – or might already be being built somewhere else in the business.

"I HAVEN'T GOT TIME TO READ LOADS OF DOCUMENTATION"

BAs aren't precious about producing reams and reams of documentation. Often such documents are stipulated by project governance processes rather than BAs themselves, but the Business Analyst should always consider their audience and the purpose of the documentation.

For example, a large collection of requirements can be split into several sub documents, each tailored to the particular audience if appropriate. On other projects, the only documentation needed may be one or two pages at a time.

BAs may also spend time with you to walk through the key points of their output, rather than throw a document at you. A good BA always includes plenty of pictures too...

"Business Analysts are just about requirements, then they move on"

If this is ever the case, it's generally against their will. BAs can add a lot of value throughout the life of a project, from helping to evaluate the design to helping the business users write acceptance tests. They can also help produce benefit realisation plans.

A BA can be particularly valuable at the concept or idea stage, clearly defining the problem and putting boundaries around it. They can also perform feasibility studies to assess delivery options upfront and save time and cost further down the line.

Basically anything that involves understanding the needs and desired benefits of the business will benefit from having a BA involved.

"All that upfront analysis costs money. Let's just build something"

Whilst there have been several studies proving that upfront analysis **saves** money, it's often hard to convince anyone that they shouldn't just "get on with it" and start building something rather than worry about thinking about what they really need. Sometimes this is the right thing to do; the question is really one of risk.

– are you likely to break anything?
– do you need to hook into any existing systems?
– will negative publicity result if things do go wrong?
– beyond a business case, do you have a clear idea of the value that the proposed change will deliver to the business?
– can you justify the costs of putting things right if they do go wrong?
– are you happy to throw away what you do produce if it proves ineffective or unsupportable?

If jumping straight in is the right answer, then a useful middle ground can be a prototyping stage. This involves working with a BA and some technical resource to quickly understand your requirements and develop a model of what you need. This can be evolved and effectively becomes a working demonstration of your requirements which can then be used as the basis for a full scale development later on.

The business gets some of what it needs quickly, the requirements get understood quicker than through documentation and business risk is minimised.

This approach won't suit every project but it's worth considering and is another demonstration that there's more to Business Analysis than requirements documents.

A bit more about requirements

Whilst there's a lot more to Business Analysis than just producing requirements, it's probably the most common situation where you'll come into contact with a BA.

But what are they and why do we need to worry about them?

Put simply, requirements are the expression of business needs in clear, unambiguous terms. Generally they will need to be communicated via some sort of documentation to anyone involved with producing a solution for them. Verbal communication can work in some situations as well but most of the time something will need to be written down.

They need to be clear and unambiguous so that you get what you actually need rather than what someone has assumed you need. They also need to be prioritised relative to each other so that the really critical ones have the most attention given to them. They also need to be uniquely identified so that they can be tracked – and the BA needs to know where the requirement came from so that they can clarify any details in future.

Capturing a set of requirements is not necessarily a one off exercise. Business requirements can be expressed at a number of different levels of detail, which are ultimately used for different purposes.

For example:

level	requirement	purpose
0	Capture data protection opt in preferences for customers	Express the business need at a high level to agree why a project is needed
1	Change the business process to accommodate capture of the data protection opt in	Express what needs to be changed so the effort to change it can be estimated
2	Automatically check claim forms for eligibility issues.	Express a particular element of functionality so that a solution can be designed
3	The tax rate must be 20%	Express a specific variable or piece of functionality so that a solution can be built

The capture, analysis and expression of these requirement levels will vary across different projects. Not every project will require all levels to be expressed – the project team should determine what is necessary at each stage.

The elicitation, analysis and expression of these requirement levels will vary across different projects. Not every project will require all levels to be expressed – the project team should determine what is necessary at each stage.

For example, at an early stage of a project it is important to express the broad scope of activity in order to gain estimates, with the aim of deciding if the project is financially viable or in fact possible from a delivery perspective. This scope will typically be expressed by level 1 requirements.

However, when specifying exactly what needs to be built, more detail is required by the person who's actually doing the building work. This is when level 2 or level 3 requirements would be needed.

Typically, level 1 requirements go through analysis in order for them to be detailed at a lower level and to understand the impacts of these requirements on other aspects of the project. This could include further discussions with the providers of the requirements, or the use of different techniques to express them in a clear, unambiguous way.

If we consider a building analogy, the Business Analyst can be thought of as the Architect.*

If you were to commission a house, an Architect will ask you what sort of house you want. What features it should have. What you intend to use it for (for example, raising a family or as a holiday home). How it should be heated. How many people intend to live there.

* Confusingly (for this analogy at least) there is often another role involved called the IT Architect – this role is responsible for the high level design and determining which "materials" should be used

They will assess the impact of your needs on the surrounding environment and provide sketches to make sure that they've understood your needs correctly. These sketches will be elaborated upon to provide technical details and be used to clearly communicate your needs to a builder.

You'd be unlikely to go straight to the builder and tell them what you want.

In the world of business, a Business Analyst will ask similar questions, and use similar techniques, to understand and communicate what the business needs to those who will build a solution for it.

Dealing with change

It's not just capturing and documenting them though. Requirements need to be **managed** throughout their life. The main reason for this is change.

People change their minds. Businesses change. Markets change.

When a project can run anywhere from one month to three years plus, it's inevitable that some things will change that affect that project – and your requirements will need to change too.

Business Analysts are responsible for assessing the impacts that any such changes have on the requirements to make sure that everyone is working to an accurate and common blueprint.

A bad requirement...

> *"CUSTOMERS SHOULD BE ABLE TO SELECT PRODUCTS FROM A DROP DOWN MENU"*

So what's wrong with this?

Well, what is the actual requirement? Is it that customers have the full range of products to choose from? Or is it that they should only be able to select one product at a time? Both are features of a drop down menu – but they have different implications. Specifying "drop down menu" upfront makes it unclear what is actually needed, and constrains the design.

If the requirement wasn't that customers should only be able to select one product at a time, and in fact the business wants them to select multiple products, then stating the solution in the requirement will result in something being delivered that's not fit for purpose.

"THE DEVICE MUST BE POWERED BY A SINGLE AA BATTERY"

This is certainly specific – but is it a good requirement?

Not really – the real requirement here is possibly for a user replaceable battery rather than it specifically needing to be an AA. More than this though, this type of requirement introduces significant limitations on the resulting design in terms of physical size, type of circuitry and even safety – AA batteries can easily leak.

Again, the point of understanding the pure business requirement is not one of pedantry – it can have serious implications for the resulting design that not only inhibit creativity within that design but can have an impact on the customer experience and ultimately the success of that product.

I want a 4 bedroom house. With a garden, and a garage

OK, we'll get to work...

◆ ◆ ◆

How's the house?

Terrible! It's expensive to heat, all the bedrooms are downstairs and the garden's far too big!

Didn't we build what you asked for...?

A brief note on testing

Testing is something that not many business users are aware of until they're asked to sign off a project. However., it's worth becoming aware of the different types of tests and how important they are. As systems and businesses themselves become more and more complex, testing becomes one of the most important things you can do.

Unit testing makes sure that the bit of code that has just been written does what it's supposed to.

System testing checks whether or not that bit of code works in the context of the overall system.

Integration testing checks that the functionality of that code works when combined with other systems.

Regression testing makes sure that the new bit of code hasn't broken any existing functionality.

All of these types of test rely on having some frame of reference that describes what you actually want so that you you can check that what has been built does the job.

If this frame of reference is flawed, then you can't really have any confidence in the testing, or have any confidence in the finished product. Worse still, you'll spend more money fixing the product after the build is complete.

Unambiguous, testable requirements are therefore key to successful (and cost-effective) business change. BAs know this, and are experienced in expressing requirements in a testable way.

For example:

<u>Untestable</u> The new home page should load as quickly as the old home page

<u>Testable</u> The new home page should load within 20ms

"THEY'RE ALL MUST-HAVES!"

A brief note on prioritisation

Your Business Analyst will at some stage need to discuss prioritisation with you. Whilst they appreciate that everything you've asked for is important (otherwise why would you ask for it...) but it's critical that the development teams understand the relative priority of your requirements.

Which requirements absolutely, positively **have** to be delivered in order for the system to be viable and your business case benefits to be realised? Which requirements will result in unwelcome regulatory attention if not delivered, or impact market perception of your brand? These are the true "must-haves" – the ones that can not get missed, no matter what.

There are many different ways of prioritising requirements, from simple 1–4 scales to more complex assessments of business value. The BA is there to help with this process and to constructively challenge your thinking – so don't be surprised or offended if your verdict of "must–have" is occasionally met with a response of "really?".

Prioritisation doesn't necessarily mean that you won't get something delivered, but it does mean that the genuinely critical ones get the most attention. In reality, projects often are time pressured and whether it's in the design, build or test stages, you want to make sure that the **really** important ones get the full attention they deserve.

To make prioritisation easier, it helps to start with the requirements that will result in your business case being unachievable if they're not met and those that will result in a financial impact if they're not met (regulatory fines for example). These are your real "must–haves". Then compare all your other requirements against these to come up with their relative importance.

It's not just IT

Business Analysts aren't just restricted to technology related change. They can also express business problems relating to processes or organisational structures.

For example, a company may have 3 different contact centres and want to reduce costs. A BA would identify the similarities and differences between the 3 centres in terms of processes, staffing, costs and locations (as well as systems) in order to fairly evaluate each one against the desired target state.

BAs understand the impacts of a change across an organisation and can express business needs relating to processes, operating models or systems.

For example, in the situation where a merger or acquisition results in two teams that need to be combined.

As with an IT change, the BA will abstract the problem:

– what processes are supported by the team now?
– what processes will need to be supported in the future?
– how many people perform each role?
– what is the ratio of "managers" to "workers"?
– how are they measured?
– how do teams interface with other teams within the organisation?

These questions will help the BA to produce abstract models of the as–is and to–be organisation and thereby drive out specific requirements that the new organisation needs to fulfil.

So what does a Business Analyst do again?

They *investigate* business problems.

They *analyse* and *abstract* those problems.

They *link* problems to *benefits*.

They *communicate* those problems to those who can resolve them.

They make sure that the business is *doing the right thing*.

They *facilitate* business change – that is, they *make business change easier*.

Without them, there is increased cost, increased business risk, lower quality and dissatisfied customers.

BAs help businesses *get* what they *really need*.

Many thanks to the following who took the time to proof–read and review this book:

Simon da Silva
Phil Bailey
Adrian Reed
Sarah Sparey
Sam Butterworth
Thomas Hewitt

pragnalysis.com is a community website dedicated to free business analysis resources – from templates, articles and blogs to a free requirements management tool.

It is entirely produced by Business Analysts, for Business Analysts.

All comments and feedback on this book gratefully received via joe@pragnalysis.com

© 2011 Joseph da Silva

What is a Business Analyst? by Joseph da Silva is licensed under a Creative Commons Attribution-NonCommercial-ShareAlike 3.0 Unported License http://creativecommons.org/licenses/by-nc-sa/3.0/

Proof

8837203R0

Made in the USA
Charleston, SC
18 July 2011